CELEBRATING THE NAME JACOB

Celebrating the Name Jacob

Walter the Educator

Silent King Books

SILENT KING BOOKS

SKB

Copyright © 2024 by Walter the Educator

All rights reserved. No part of this book may be reproduced in any manner whatsoever without written permission except in the case of brief quotations embodied in critical articles and reviews.

First Printing, 2024

Disclaimer
This book is a literary work; poems are not about specific persons, locations, situations, and/or circumstances unless mentioned in a historical context. This book is for entertainment and informational purposes only. The author and publisher offer this information without warranties expressed or implied. No matter the grounds, neither the author nor the publisher will be accountable for any losses, injuries, or other damages caused by the reader's use of this book. The use of this book acknowledges an understanding and acceptance of this disclaimer.

dedicated to everyone with the first name of Jacob

JACOB

Echoes dance with glee,

JACOB

Resounds a name, beloved decree.

JACOB

Jacob, the beacon, in shadows bright,

JACOB

Ignites the sky with its celestial might.

JACOB

In whispers soft, through leafy glades,

JACOB

His name cascades in serenades.

JACOB

A symphony of consonants and vowels,

JACOB

In every breeze, his essence prowls.

JACOB

From ancient tomes, his story told,

JACOB

In ink of gold, his legend bold.

JACOB

A shepherd once, amidst the flock,

JACOB

Yet destiny called, no ticking clock.

JACOB

In dreams, he wrestled with the divine,

JACOB

Beneath the stars, where destinies entwine.

JACOB

Jacob, the seeker, in the night's embrace,

JACOB

Found solace in that sacred space.

JACOB

A ladder tall, to heavens soared,

JACOB

Where angels sang, and mysteries roared.

JACOB

His name engraved on celestial spheres,

JACOB

A testament to faith through fears.

JACOB

In twilight's glow, where shadows play,

JACOB

Jacob's name holds sway.

JACOB

A symbol of resilience, steadfast and true,

JACOB

In every trial, his spirit grew.

JACOB

Through deserts vast and oceans wide,

JACOB

His name endured, a beacon guide.

JACOB

In wilderness, where hopes grow dim,

JACOB

Jacob's light burns ever within.

JACOB

In bustling streets and silent halls,

JACOB

His name resounds, the echo calls.

JACOB

A reminder of strength in every stride,

JACOB

A compass true in life's wild ride.

JACOB

Jacob, the name that echoes through time,

JACOB

In every heart, a sacred chime.

JACOB

A melody of courage and grace,

JACOB

In every soul, finds its rightful place.

JACOB

So let us raise our voices high,

JACOB

To Jacob's name, let echoes fly.

JACOB

For in its sound, we find our kin,

JACOB

A bond unbroken, through thick and thin.

JACOB

In valleys low and mountains high,

JACOB

Jacob's name shall never die.

JACOB

A testament to the human soul,

JACOB

In every triumph, in every goal.

JACOB

ABOUT THE CREATOR

Walter the Educator is one of the pseudonyms for Walter Anderson. Formally educated in Chemistry, Business, and Education, he is an educator, an author, a diverse entrepreneur, and he is the son of a disabled war veteran. "Walter the Educator" shares his time between educating and creating. He holds interests and owns several creative projects that entertain, enlighten, enhance, and educate, hoping to inspire and motivate you.

Follow, find new works, and stay up to date with Walter the Educator™ at WaltertheEducator.com

www.ingramcontent.com/pod-product-compliance
Lightning Source LLC
LaVergne TN
LVHW010619070526
838199LV00063BA/5201